JAMES DEAN

A Life From Beginning to End

Copyright © 2018 by Hourly History.

All rights reserved.

small role as the Apostle John and only had a few lines in the piece.

Despite the small amount of lines in the production, Dean gained a cult following from perhaps an unlikely source—a local Catholic girls' school. The film had apparently become a part of the school's curriculum, and Dean had received recognition as a kind of heartthrob. For his work on the TV special, he was also able to meet his end of the rent, receiving a check for $150. With this initial success, Dean decided to forego his studies to pursue acting full time.

Table of Contents

Introduction
Losing His Family
A Troubled Childhood
Dean's First Big Breaks
Friends and Lovers
The Rehearsal Club
Working on a Yacht
Breakthroughs and Heartbreaks
The Real Rebel Rouser
Dean's Acting and Car Racing Career
The Final Ride
Conclusion

the little boy that she loved him, his mother went to great lengths to demonstrate it by constantly playing with him and showing him attention. So much so that she was sometimes criticized by onlookers who believed her to be babying her son, to which she would protest, "He's all that I have! And I love him!"

When Dean was six years old, his father moved the family all the way to Santa Monica, California. Winton Dean had come from a family of farmers in Indiana but wished to free himself from that fate, and so had his family leave the drudgery of the farm behind so that he could attend dental school in California. James Dean's father was gone quite a bit during this period, so he and his mother often found themselves alone together and grew even closer as a result.

It is said that to entertain themselves they would often create elaborate plays and act them out among each other. Dean's mother often remarked that James was everything to her, and James, in his young life, no doubt felt the same. But tragically enough, the time the two would have together would be cut short when his mother became afflicted with a rapid onset of uterine cancer. After a brief struggle, she passed away. She was 29 years old, and James Dean was only 9.

It's often hard for children to comprehend the finality of death, and the true impact is usually felt years later. This was apparently the case with James Dean. He was fairly quiet and stoic at his mother's funeral, but the heartache over her loss would build with each passing day, and the sadness of her untimely death would come to haunt him for the rest of his life.

Chapter Two

A Troubled Childhood

"I'm a serious-minded and intense little devil, terribly gauche and so tense I don't see how people stay in the same room with me. I know I wouldn't tolerate myself."

—James Dean

After his mother's passing, James Dean's father who had always relegated most of the duty of parenting to his wife, found himself quickly overwhelmed with the prospect of being a single parent. Feeling that he would be unable to juggle his career and parenting, he asked family members if they could help him shoulder the burden. Winton's sister, Ortense, answered his call.

Ortense was married to a man named Marcus Winslow, and they lived on a farm in Fairmount, Indiana. This piece of small-town America would later become famously associated with the acting legend of James Dean, and to this very day if you drive through the area, you will see signs of this legacy posted all over the town. But besides the signs and markers, the town of Fairmount hasn't changed a whole lot, and now, as in the time of James Dean, it remains mostly farmland.

Dean's newly adopted parents were devoutly religious and somewhat strict, but despite some of the severity of their habits, they were open and loving towards the young boy. Marcus especially took an interest in Dean and, since he had no biological son at the time, was ready to confer all of the rewards of sonship onto James Dean. All of this love and support no doubt made the move, his mother's untimely death, and the separation from his father much easier to tolerate.

Here Dean lived an idyllic life on the farm, taking care of crops and animals, as well as having plenty of play time for himself. Marcus built a swing set for the boy, and during the summer months, he would even convert the old family barn into a makeshift gymnasium. Here, Dean and his uncle would have the time of their life, playing, laughing, and engaging in all manner of acrobatic maneuvers. Dean's love of engaging in physical stunts is said to stem from this experience.

As he grew older, however, he began to feel painfully out of place, not only in his adoptive family but the whole Fairmount community at large. Dean did not feel like he belonged in farm-town America, and as he became a teenager, he longed to escape the cornfields of Northern Indiana altogether. His first taste of something different came when a pastor and local mentor took him to the state capital of Indianapolis to see a running of the Indianapolis 500.

The 500 Formula One race track was the one claim to fame the state of Indiana had, and James Dean was fascinated. And not just by the roaring engines of the race cars but the diverse audience of spectators seated all around him. Sitting with his mentor in nosebleed seats inside a race track built more like the ancient Roman Colosseum, Dean felt strangely at home.

In the rush and roar of the cars below, Dean felt like he had finally escaped—even if just briefly—the monotony of rural Indiana life. His pastor, a local Methodist minister named James DeWeerd, knew that Dean was looking to expand his horizons, and he was interested in exposing the young Dean to new experiences. But unfortunately, some of the horizon-expanding experiences that the pastor is said to have exposed Dean to were of a much more crude and base kind.

There are several sources—including from DeWeerd himself—that the relationship between DeWeerd and the young and impressionable Dean soon turned into a predatory one. And years after Dean's death, DeWeerd admitted that he used to take him on long country rides in his convertible and park to secluded locations, where he proceeded to seduce the young man into carrying out a sexual relationship with him.

Until his death, James Dean never publicly mentioned such instances in his past. But you have to keep in mind that back in the 1950s such things were not talked about—if James Dean was a victim of a predatory relationship with an older man, it's unlikely that he would make it known. Despite the fact that he never publicly went on the record, famous actress Elizabeth Taylor claimed after Dean's death that he had indeed confided in her that he was molested by his pastor.

But at the time, Dean was stoic, and he kept all of the turmoil over the troubled relationship, the death of his mother, and his painful sense of rejection and isolation to himself. By the time he reached his senior year in high school, however, his angst would begin to come to the surface. And after his rage exploded in the form of a fist fight with another classmate, Dean—the future rebel without a cause—was expelled.

Chapter Three

Dean's First Big Breaks

"I don't want anything seventy-thirty. Fifty-fifty's always good enough for me. I don't want to have to give anybody seventy; I don't want anybody to give seventy. I want fifty."

—James Dean

After being expelled from his high school, James Dean was eventually reinstated and did manage to walk across the stage with his graduating class of 1949. Even so, he knew that his future lay elsewhere, and as soon as his high school diploma was in his hands, he was seeking a means to leave Fairmount, Indiana behind. His opportunity came in the form of a letter from his long absentee father, Winton.

His dad had remarried and created a new life for himself in California since leaving his son in the care of his sister and was now expressing a desire for his son to join him on the West Coast. Dean would long harbor a grudge against his father for not playing a more active role in his childhood, but being the pragmatist that he was, when his dad extended the offer for him to stay with him in Los Angeles, he couldn't refuse it. This was his ticket out of small-town Indiana for good.

Upon arrival, his initial plan was to attend UCLA and take courses in acting. Throughout middle school and high school, Dean had taken part in drama classes and theatrical productions, and he had a keen interest in the arts. He felt that majoring in acting at UCLA would help him to determine if he had any chance of making it in show business. But his father—like many fathers tend to do—wished for his son to pursue more practical endeavors and encouraged him to attend Santa Monica City College as a pre-law student.

It seems that after a few go-rounds between the two over just who knew best for James Dean's life, the deciding factor that swayed the young man was when his father brought home a used 1939 Chevy Sedan and offered to give it to him on the condition that he pursue his studies at Santa Monica. Dean acquiesced, but even though he agreed to go to Santa Monica City College as a pre-law student, he secretly enrolled in as many drama and theatre based electives as he could. It was in one of these elective art courses that Dean gained the attention of Gene Owen, who at the time was the chair of the school's theatre department.

Gene contacted Dean and invited him to start participating in dramatic readings for a student radio production course. One of Dean's first assignments was to do a reading of Edgar Allan Poe's melancholy *The Tell-Tale Heart*. Soon after this production, he was recruited to take part in a production of Shakespeare's *Hamlet*. With these major works under his belt early on in his academia, Dean soon became well known on campus as a budding actor in his own right. And towards the end of the semester when Dean brought home a somewhat lackluster report card, with A's in Drama but C's in just about everything else, his father finally allowed him to enroll at UCLA.

Dean also wished to leave the confines of his father's apartment and decided to join a fraternity house on campus. But things didn't start out too well for him. Then, as now, fraternities tended to request new pledges to go through ordeals known as initiations. Dean's initiation was so strenuous that it almost killed him. He was made to lay down at the bottom of a swimming pool filled with water. The idea was for him to hold his breath and lay down on the big drainage vent at the bottom of the pool. His fraternity brothers would then hit the switch that would suck all the water out of the swimming pool as Dean attempted to swim against the current and out of the water. Suffice it to say this ill-hatched scheme didn't work out quite as planned.

The whirlpool current proved to be too strong, and Dean became trapped at the bottom of the pool. He was unable to escape the suction at the bottom and began to drown. Once his panicked fraternity brothers realized what was happening, they jumped in to drag him out. And this wasn't enough for Dean—a fellow fraternity brother criticized him for his strong interest in the arts and derided him as a "fruit." It was only after this crude remark that James Dean decided enough was enough, and after punching the frat boy in the nose, he left the fraternity for good.

He found lodging with a classmate named Bill Bast, who was renting an apartment in Santa Monica for $300 a month. Dean then began his acting career in earnest and starred in local commercials such as a stint in an advertisement for Pepsi in which a young James Dean can be seen decked out in a sailor's uniform singing the Pepsi jingle of the day, "Live it up with Pepsi-Cola." These commercials were for experience and name recognition as Dean sought to build his portfolio.

For his efforts in the Pepsi commercial, Dean was paid the paltry amount of 10 dollars, which was next to nothing even in the 1950s. As modest of a start as this was, it was in this appearance that Dean would first meet two of his future co-stars for his epic film *Rebel Without a Cause*.

But the first break that this commercial debut would provide for Dean was a TV Easter special called *Hill Number One*. The plot of the show centered around a group of U.S. soldiers attempting to take a hill from enemy soldiers. The fighting is rough, and the group soon grows tired and needs to rest. During this respite, the chaplain steps forward and makes the observation to the troops, "War is a crucifixion." Shortly after this statement, the film sequence flashes backward in time to the crucifixion of Christ, in which Pilate and Nicodemus are being portrayed as discussing what to do with Christ's body on a hill that is presumably supposed to represent Mt. Golgotha where, according to Christian tradition, Christ is said to have been crucified. James Dean played a

Introduction

James Dean is known as the first rebel. He was a '50s-styled, leather-clad biker rebuking authority. With his black turtleneck and a penchant for bongo drums and poetry, he could also easily be a kind of forerunner to the beatniks. And with his often unkempt, wild hair and far-reaching philosophies, he is often cited as a kind of early hippie as well. But whatever category you put him in, James Dean was the embodiment of cool.

He had a cool look, cool clothes, cool attitude, and a cool backstory that most know nothing about. James Dean began life in Indiana as the descendant of a long line of farmers. After the tragic passing of his mother at a young age and the virtual abandonment of his father, he was left to be raised by his sister and her husband on a farm in Fairmount, Indiana.

So just how did this Indiana farm boy become a Hollywood legend and kickstart a counterculture rebellion that would last throughout the '50s, '60s, and beyond? Who was James Dean? Come along as we find out more about the man, the legend, and the eternal rebel without a cause: James Dean.

Chapter One

Losing His Family

"Studying cows, pigs and chickens can help an actor develop his character. There are a lot of things I learned from animals. One was that they couldn't hiss or boo me."

—James Dean

James Byron Dean was born in the sleepy Northern Indiana town of Marion on February 8, 1931. James was the only child of Winton Dean and Mildred Marie Wilson. As a child, James lived with his parents in a small, modest apartment.

The Dean family didn't have much money, but whatever extra cash they did have was usually spent showering young James with gifts. His father would later recall his son going through his toys rather quickly. He would be excited about them for a few days before losing interest and wishing to move on to something new. This quickness to move on to the next big adventure would in many ways come to embody the spirit of the rest of his life. James Dean would later be known to have a manic interest in certain subjects for days on end, only to cast it to the side at a moment's notice.

Besides material gifts, his mother bestowed upon Dean a strong kinship and sense of love. Besides telling

Chapter Four

Friends and Lovers

"An actor must interpret life, and in order to do so must be willing to accept all the experiences life has to offer. In fact, he must seek out more of life than life puts at his feet."

—James Dean

Along with his acting pursuits, Dean soon became acquainted with his first serious girlfriend during this period. He began to date Beverly Wills, the daughter of the famed comedian Joan Davis. In Dean, Beverly saw a kindred spirit and someone who was truly passionate about life. But there was one problem: Beverly was already Dean's roommate's girlfriend. The two had begun secretly seeing each other behind Bill's back.

And as Bill Bast would later recall, he only found out when the two showed up at his workplace to give him a ride home. It was a bit of a curious sight to see them together, and as Bill piled into the car, Beverly suddenly announced, "Bill there is something I have to tell you—" She then motioned toward James Dean and promptly informed him, "We're in love." Bill was more than a little shocked at this proclamation, but initially, he didn't show any outward hostility toward the newfound couple.

It wasn't until a few days later when Bill abruptly moved out of the apartment that his agitation was made known. Without his roommate there to pay the other half of the rent, Dean had no choice but to find lodging elsewhere.

He was working part-time parking cars in the parking lot of LA's CBS studio when he just happened to meet Rogers Brackett, an executive and radio director for a prominent advertising firm based out of New York. After Dean explained his desire to break out in the industry and his need for a place to stay, Mr. Brackett was more than willing to oblige. It is alleged that—as with his relationship with the pastor in Fairmount—this older man soon began a sexual relationship with James Dean. Brackett himself would later reminisce about their pairing, stating, "If it was a father and son relationship, it was also incestuous."

At any rate, Brackett proved to be quite good for Dean's career, not only giving him a stable place to stay but also providing him with the connections he so desperately needed. Because of Brackett, Dean was able to get several bit parts on TV, radio, and film.

In October 1951, Brackett took Dean with him to New York when he was called upon to direct a radio show. Here in New York, Brackett paid for Dean to stay at the Iroquois Hotel on West Forty-Fourth Street, near Times Square. Dean was now right in the thick of all the excitement and drama that the world of New York theatre had to offer—both on and off the stage.

New York was a mecca for TV actors in those days, and directors would often hold mass auditions called cattle calls in which they could quickly survey hundreds of actors at a time. It was during one of these cattle calls that Dean would meet one of the friends he would have for the rest of his life: Martin Landau. Landau was at this time a struggling yet promising actor. The two began to hang out around the city together and exchanged numbers, hoping to stay in touch for some time to come.

Years after Dean's untimely demise, Landau would recall, "Jimmy [James Dean] often said that he had to make it as an actor while he was young." He then added somewhat ominously, "Sometimes we talked about the possibility of dying young but we never thought that would happen to us." But Dean did have a do-or-die attitude, and Landau had no idea of just how prescient his conversation with Dean would one day become.

Chapter Five

The Rehearsal Club

"Being an actor is the loneliest thing in the world. You are all alone with your concentration and imagination, and that's all you have."

—James Dean

In his free time, Dean was fond of hanging out in the downstairs lounge of the Rehearsal Club. The Rehearsal Club was a dormitory-style apartment reserved for young actresses and dancers trying to make it big in New York. For Dean and his male peers, it was also the perfect place to meet women. And so it was when James Dean met the next major female presence in his life, Elizabeth "Dizzy" Sheridan. It all started when he was seated right across from her in the lobby of the Rehearsal Club.

Dean was lounging on a couch sifting through magazines when Dizzy caught his eye. Then suddenly Dean read aloud a passage he was reading, proclaiming in a funny voice, "I admit in retrospect that my methods were unorthodox to say the least." It took Dizzy a second to realize it, but then it struck her that Dean was sarcastically chastising himself for a pickup line he never even made. Unable to resist the goofy, offbeat humor, Dizzy played along reading a line of her own from a magazine she had, and soon the two were laughing at each other.

Dean, seizing his moment of good humor, then asked her if she would like to get a couple of drinks with him at an Italian Bar and Restaurant down the street from them called Jerry's. Intrigued by the amusing character, Dizzy agreed, and the two quickly fell for each other. To make things official, they soon decided to get a place of their own and checked into a room at the Hargrave Hotel. The room was modest to the extreme, and the space of the room that they shared together was described as being the size of a broom closet.

Even so, Dean, whose acting parts had slowed down considerably, was embarrassed to find that he couldn't carry his share of the rent, making Dizzy foot most of the bill. Dean didn't have money for food, basic necessities, or even bus fare most of the time, so when his old friend Brackett came calling once again and offered to let Dean stay with him, he jumped at the chance. He explained the situation to Dizzy, and she reluctantly agreed, and although the two would remain close, they lived separately.

Bracket, stepping back into the role of mentor, promised Dean that he was going to really show him around town this time. And one of the places he directed the aspiring actor to was the Hallmark Company in which the *Hallmark Hall of Fame* weekly telecasts were produced. Hallmark created regular TV dramas in which Dean hoped to be cast, but at first the best Brackett's connections could do for him was give him a regular gig as a background tech tasked with displaying the final credits.

The gig entailed Dean standing at a blackboard and writing the credits by hand, as the camera zoomed in on the words he scrawled on the board. This sounds pretty strange to most of us today, but keep in mind that in the early days of TV in the 1950s, computerized graphics and text was not available, leading many programs to improvise just like this. Although the job didn't allow him any real screen time, it did provide him with a steady, weekly paycheck for his efforts.

Along with his duties on the set of Hallmark, he was soon able to branch out and act again by way of a radio program called the *U.S. Steel Radio Hour*. In the program, he gained a supporting role as the friend of Abraham Lincoln in a historical drama called "Prologue to Glory." Dean was now six months into his stint in New York, and things were looking up. It was in this triumphant state of mind that Dean received a phone call from his old roomie and fellow thespian back in California, Bill Blast.

Bill had stuck it out and graduated from UCLA while Dean was making his way in New York, and he was now eager to be reunited with his old film school buddy. Whatever angst or animosity the two may have had in the past had dissolved, and as soon as Bill arrived Dean began showing him the ropes. Dean was the veteran now, and Bill was the fresh-faced newbie taking in the sights of an unfamiliar city.

Things had come full circle, and Bill took note of how much Dean had changed. He saw him now in a much different light than he did the timid young man who had been fresh off the farms of Indiana. James Dean had come into his own and was quickly rising in the ranks as he climbed New York's social ladder. Dean, the film school dropout, seemed poised for superstardom, where Bill Blast, the UCLA graduate, had given up on dreams of acting long ago.

Bill, at this point in his life, was content to utilize his new degree from UCLA to work behind the scenes in production. He fulfilled this by securing a job for himself with CBS Studios working as one of the hired hands in the communications department. Dean meanwhile was determined to further his acting ambition by auditioning for NYC's prestigious Actors Studio, which at the time was being headed by the living legends of Lee Strasberg and Elia Kazan.

After performing a brief skit with a friend of his, Dean was accepted. This was a momentous event for him. And in a letter dated 1952 sent back home to his folks in Fairmount, Indiana, a 21-year-old James Dean described his big break as "the best thing that can happen to an actor."

Chapter Six

Working on a Yacht

"To grasp the full significance of life is the actor's duty; to interpret it his problem; and to express it his dedication."

—James Dean

As well as things were going for Dean, as the summer of 1952 was winding down, he found his prospects for employment slowing down. In July 1952, the Hallmark Company took its annual break in programming, not to restart until the following fall. Even with his impressive resume and portfolio of experience, Dean found himself barely scraping by. Around this time, Dean's old flame Dizzy came back into town and convinced him to come with her to Ocean City, New Jersey where she had been working.

Dean tried his luck on the Jersey Shore but soon grew bored and wandered on back to New York. From here he tried out for a leading role in a TV drama called *Life with Father*, but he wasn't able to land the role. Fearing yet another rejection, Dean then reluctantly auditioned for a role in the epic *Oklahoma!*, a film adaptation of the popular musical of the same name that had been in the works for a while. Dean was ultimately rejected for this production as well, but it wasn't a complete loss.

He managed to meet a powerful friend in the form of Paul Newman, who was already an up and coming actor. Dean's luck began to turn when he was given a position as a deckhand on a yacht. This may seem like an unlikely way to break out in the film industry, but this wasn't just any yacht. The yacht carried Lemuel Ayers, a screenwriter who was working on a new production for Broadway called *See the Jaguar*.

Dean helped with duties on the deck of Ayers' yacht when, on the way to Martha's Vineyard, they sailed right into a bad storm. Ayers was apparently so impressed with Dean's ability as a sailor that he informed him that he would consider casting him for a role for *See the Jaguar* as soon as they returned stateside. But after several weeks had gone by without any word from Ayers, Dean grew impatient with waiting and decided to hitchhike with his best friends Bill and Dizzy all the way to Fairmont, Indiana, to relax, reminisce, and gather his thoughts.

They took a bus to the New Jersey Turnpike before hitchhiking to Pennsylvania. In Pennsylvania, they bumped into a baseball player for the Pittsburgh Pirates, Clyde McCullough, who was traveling to Iowa. Clyde, an amiable enough character, agreed to drop Dean and his friends off in Fairmount, Indiana on his way over there. The group then arrived safe and sound and were dropped off just outside of Fairmount, walking the rest of the way to Dean's family farm.

Dean received a warm reception, and his friends were treated as if they were part of the family. Here the group could relax in warm beds and count on a steady diet of cooked meals. Dean and his friends passed the next few days with Dean's loving Aunt Ortense and Uncle Marcus. The only thing that was able to pull Dean out of their comforting embrace was a sudden call from New York informing him that production for *See the Jaguar* was slated to begin immediately.

After an early Thanksgiving dinner that his aunt insisted upon, Dean and his friends hightailed it back to New York City. Dean then threw himself headlong into the rehearsal process of the production. The plot of this piece was rather unique, dealing with a young man who had been virtually imprisoned his whole life by his deranged mother. Upon her death, the socially awkward youth was forced to come to grips with the world around him that he had been sheltered from.

It was a role that—in many ways—James Dean could understand, drawing upon his own innate feelings of insecurity and of being an outsider. At first, it seemed like it was destined to be, and everything was coming together. But when the production opened on Broadway on December 3, 1952, it soon became clear that the opposite was true. The characters from a writing perspective were ill-defined with behaviors that seemed incredibly dark, without any justification from the plot as to why their dealings would be so nefarious.

As one critic from the *Daily News* put it, the play was "lovely to see and hear, but it makes no sense." The cast presented a spectacular show of theatrics, but to many who witnessed it, they appeared to be a bunch of overzealous actors screaming at the top of their lungs for no apparent reason. These were the most frequent criticisms of the play as a whole.

But even though much of the storyline of the production seemed incomprehensible to those who saw it, Dean managed to stand out and received high marks for his incredible acting ability—even if it was misplaced in a poorly written screenplay. A review in the *Herald Tribune* described Dean's efforts as adding "an extraordinary performance in an almost impossible role."

James Dean was given the honorable distinction of having gone above and beyond to make the best of a badly written script. And thanks to his standout performance in what was otherwise a complete box office failure, as 1952 turned into 1953, James Dean would soon be the talk of the town.

Chapter Seven

Breakthroughs and Heartbreaks

"A lot of the time with an independent production, you go onto the set, and you rehearse it in front of the crew, and at that point, the cinematographer takes over. You start accommodating the camera instead of the camera accommodating you."

—Martin Landau

After gaining fame for his work in *See the Jaguar*, Dean was hired to reprise a dramatic role for the *Kate Smith Variety Show* where Dean played the part of the son of a moonshine distiller at odds with the law. Then in February, Dean was cast in a TV production called the *Capture of Jesse James*, another historical piece in which he played the part of one of Jesse James captors. Dean's character ends up shooting Jesse James in the back. The episode aired on Dean's 22nd birthday, and he took this to be a good omen of its success.

With all of his recent work, Dean now had enough money to forego his communal living with friends and other actors and put himself up in his own room once again in the Iroquois Hotel. This led to his main group of friends, Dizzy and Bill Bast, to go their separate ways. Dizzy got a job as a dancer in St. Thomas, and Bill left for Hollywood to pursue screenwriting. Bereft of his closest confidants, Dean now threw himself completely into his work.

Fast becoming a jack of all trades, Dean appeared frequently in TV land in anthology series such as *Kraft Television Theatre*, *Robert Montgomery Presents*, and *General Electric Theatre*. It was all of this name recognition that eventually led to him being cast in the role of Cal in the film *East of Eden*. The plot of the film takes place in the 1910s and follows the lives of two families that have lived side by side for generations in Southern California.

Dean scored the part of Cal Trask on April 8, 1954. As soon as he was given the go-ahead, Dean left New York for Los Angeles to begin work. He always prided himself on his ability to improve, and the production team for *East of Eden* wished to allow this rare skill to flourish unhindered. And incredibly enough, a lot of Dean's performance on *East of Eden* was adlibbed, or improvised.

This freedom enabled Dean to utilize the full depths of his dark emotion on screen and would set the stage for his future performance in *Rebel Without a Cause*. *East of Eden* received rave reviews and would eventually have Dean nominated (posthumously) for an Academy Award for Best Actor. Filming for *East of Eden* began in May, and most of the production was set to take place in Salinas Valley in California, with some other locations being marked out for Mendocino and San Francisco.

To celebrate his newfound role, Dean bought a vehicle that would become synonymous with his legacy: a Triumph T110 motorcycle. Knowing how reckless of a driver that Dean was, the director of *East of Eden* quickly informed him that if he wanted to continue production on his film, he needed to park the motorcycle and forego riding during the rest of filming.

In a foreshadowing of things to come, Kazan stated at the time, "If he had to kill himself, I'd rather not have him to do it during my movie." Fortunately, Dean took this piece of advice and avoided any major mishap. In the meantime, he had found a new thrill in his life to keep him occupied in the form of Pier Angeli, a 21-year-old Italian actress who happened to be in a production of her own on a nearby set.

Filming of *East of Eden* wrapped up in August 1954. Everything seemed to be falling into place for the film, and Dean expected it to be the breakthrough success that he needed. But right as he was on the cusp of professional greatness, he received a massive personal setback in the form of a public and messy breakup with Pier Angeli. And shortly thereafter, in October 1954, Pier announced that she was engaged to pop singer Vic Damone.

Dean is said to have been heartbroken. He is alleged to have told Pier, "Oh, no, please say you're kidding me." But she was not kidding, she was completely serious about her plans of matrimony and proceeded to get married to Vic Damone on November 24, 1954. Dean was deeply affected by what he could only feel as a betrayal of the highest order, and it's said to have affected him for the rest of his life.

Some even claimed to have seen Dean perched on his motorcycle in the church parking lot on the day of the wedding, sitting with a morose look on his face and his eyes filling with tears. He then supposedly revved his engine as if in a final farewell before thundering away. It sounds like a tragic scene out of a movie, but as always, it was Dean's personal life that held the most heart-wrenching of dramas.

Chapter Eight
The Real Rebel Rouser

"I always tried to play the bad guys as guys who didn't know they were bad guys. There are villains we run into all the time, but they don't think they are doing anything wrong. If they do, they think they are cunning and smart. When people break laws and ethical rules, they justify it in their own terms."

—Martin Landau

Dean's tour de force *East of Eden* premiered at the Astor Theatre in New York on March 9, 1955. But Dean wasn't present for the debut, he was instead going west, back to California. Almost as soon as he arrived back, he was made aware of the great fanfare and acclaim that his latest contribution to the film industry was making.

The reception of *East of Eden*'s opening night was almost all positive, and Dean was now considered a top-notch actor. As one critic put it at the time, "When the last scene faded from the Astor Theatre screen last night a new star appeared—James Dean." By the end of the month, *East of Eden* was even listed as one of Variety's top-grossing films. But Dean had an interesting way of handling this new-found praise and acclaim—most of the time he nonchalantly sloughed it off.

On one occasion for example, an adoring actress complimented him, "You're getting a lot of good publicity these days, all about your wonderful performance in *East of Eden*." As a response, Dean simply shrugged his shoulders and grunted, "Most of it is a bunch of shit." Dean seemed perfect for the role of the rebel, and while others were reveling in his success, he was openly rebelling against it.

Some have drawn parallels between Dean and early punk rock musicians, who after reaching the top of the music charts were often fond of calling their music nothing but bullshit and their fans completely worthless. Dean, scoffing at his own accomplishment, was in many ways the forefather of these progenitors of artistic self-mortification. If others wanted to make Dean into a big star, he wanted to show that he could care less, and as he told a Hollywood reporter at the time, the movie business was not the "be all end all" for him.

He wanted to make it clear that he had other interests. And one of these interests was racing. In some ways it should come as no surprise that this Indiana native, who was fascinated by the race track he once witnessed at the Indy 500, would be so enamored with fast cars. Speed spoke to him, and the rush of adrenalin it brought ameliorated his doubts and fears in ways that nothing else could. And one of the first things he did upon returning to California was to buy a brand-new Porsche Speedster.

Dean claimed at the time that this was not just a joy ride but a practical investment for the beginnings of a true racing career. And who knows? If he had managed to live more than another year after its purchase, this Indiana Hoosier just might have fulfilled that pledge. But Dean was unfortunately on the fast track to more than just Hollywood and auto racing, and many have attested to the fact that his erratic behavior was making him unstable.

His antics at the movie studios were already getting out of hand. He was said to be demanding and at times rude, and many claimed Dean was hard to work with. Dean during this period also got into the habit of being armed. On one occasion, word got out that he kept a gun stowed away with him in his dressing room. The studio executives in charge were appalled and quickly had the firearm removed. It was against this unstable backdrop that a woman, who was known in the California scene as Vampira, stepped into Dean's life.

Her real name was Maila Nurmi. She had worked as an exotic dancer before getting a gig as a Morticia Addams-styled vampire on television in the aptly titled *The Vampira Show*. The show was an anthology horror series in the same vein as *The Twilight Zone*. Dean met Vampira at a Sunset Boulevard coffee shop called Googies, which was frequented by local actors. Dean was fascinated by her and saw her offbeat character as a reflection of himself. As Vampira herself liked to describe it, they had the "same neuroses" in common.

The very first time Dean took Vampira back to his apartment, some of those neuroses were on full display. Before she left, Dean is said to have insisted on giving her a parting gift: a book by Ray Bradbury about a youth who had committed suicide by strangling himself. It was one of

Dean's favorite stories. Vampira was apparently one of the few people out there that could not only accept but also enjoy Dean's darker side.

The two soon became close friends. Dean became so comfortable with her that he even got into the habit of randomly dropping in on her. But Dean didn't see fit to use the door; instead he would climb right into her window. Oddly enough, close friends like Vampira were not the only ones that Dean forced his entry onto. Dean and another friend from Googies had gotten into the habit of snooping around neighborhoods in West Hollywood, randomly walking up to houses and attempting to open their doors.

If the door was unlocked and no one was home, they would then walk inside and pull some kind of random prank on the residents such as cooking themselves a meal or making a cup of coffee and leaving the remnants for the homeowners to find later on.

As shown by these stunts, Dean was becoming increasingly restless as he waited between films. His angst had been growing to such a fever pitch that it came as a relief to Dean—and many around him—when famed director Nicholas Ray called him to begin work on a new film. This one would find the restless youth portraying the role he seemed born for in the production of *Rebel Without a Cause*.

Chapter Nine

Dean's Acting and Car Racing Career

"When an actor plays a scene exactly the way a director orders, it isn't acting. It's following instructions. Anyone with the physical qualifications can do that."

—James Dean

Just before beginning his work on the set of *Rebel Without a Cause*, James Dean fulfilled another passion of his: being a race car driver. In early March 1955 just weeks before shooting would begin, Dean took his Porsche and entered into a motorsport match with the California Sports Cars Club in Palm Springs. It was an amateurish competition consisting of six laps over about two miles worth of track. Dean began the race in fourth place, but as soon as the signal was given to hit the accelerator, Dean gunned it and shot off, leaving the other drivers in the dust.

Dean easily maintained his lead for the duration of the race and won a silver trophy for finishing first in a victory lap that would have made the Indianapolis 500 proud. But this was just his entry into the field, and the next contest would be professional drivers only. In this competition, after a harrowing 27-lap run, Dean finished third place. His fellow drivers—while commending his effort to overcome racing veterans—abhorred what they perceived to be the incredible recklessness that he employed to achieve it.

As one of his fellow competitors put it at the time, "His skill was a dangerous one. The kind that comes from a desperate desire to win. He was a menace to himself and other drivers. He would take any kind of chance to be first." These words would prove to be yet another ominous and prescient statement in regard to James Dean and the days to come.

On March 28, immediately after his forays on the race track, Dean showed up on set for *Rebel Without a Cause* and began work on the film. Most of this film would be shot on site in Los Angeles, but a few scenes would be filmed in other locations such as a high school in Santa Monica, a prison in Hollywood, and a local planetarium; the latter of which became a favorite stomping grounds for James Dean fans after his death.

During the filming, Dean was perceived by his fellow cast as being very talented, but also very difficult. He would often leave his co-stars waiting for hours on end before shooting a scene, simply to get himself in the right mood. At one point, he is said to have locked himself in his dressing room for over an hour, playing a set of bongos and consuming a large amount of wine to psyche himself up enough to read his lines. But despite the eccentricity, it couldn't be denied that Dean managed to capture something quite magical once he was able to channel it into the dialogue of the movie. Some that knew Dean felt that he was merely letting loose enough to be himself, showing his pain and torment on the silver screen.

Even his former girlfriend Dizzy Sheridan had to do a double take after watching one of Dean's love scenes with his co-star Natalie Wood. In one part of the dialogue, Wood asks, "Is this what it is like to love somebody?" Dean then replied with a simple but sweet, "Oh wow." Dizzy could immediately recognize it as a line he had given her in their own romantic moments.

But if his close friends recognized intimate moments from Dean, the larger audience recognized something else altogether. In his defiant snarls, catchphrases, and bursts of anger, Dean managed to bottle, package, and hand deliver the eclectic mix of jumbled emotions that all American teens seemed to be feeling right back to them. This freewheeling rebel was agitated without any known cause and managed to encapsulate the feeling of a generation. The movie played up these adolescent archetypes to perfection. Even the scene where Dean's character tells a social worker to "get lost" seems to be a larger symbolism of the youth of America rebelling against the social mores of the day.

And the teenagers weren't the only ones to take notice of these themes, the parents noticed right along with them and reacted by lobbying to shut the film down. Some were successful, as was evidenced when a local censorship board in Memphis, Tennessee managed to get the movie banned outright. They claimed that it was "inimical to the public welfare" to screen the film in their town and had it shut down.

But the powers in Tennessee could not stop the smash hit that *Rebel Without a Cause* was, and Hollywood was not about to let a few dissenters in Memphis cramp their style. Soon enough, James Dean was in high demand with offers piling at his feet. But no matter how many accolades came his way, Dean was under contract with Warner Brothers, and he was obligated to fulfill it.

They already had his next role in mind. They wanted for Dean to play the part of Jett Rink, a ranch hand who struck it rich and became a millionaire. In this film titled *Giant*, Dean starred alongside acting heavyweights such as Elizabeth Taylor and Rock Hudson. This film was meant to be a coming of age for James Dean and his transition from a misanthropic teenage heartthrob to a true giant on the silver screen.

Chapter Ten

The Final Ride

"Death can't be considered because, if you're afraid to die, there's no room in your life to make discoveries."

—James Dean

It was in the middle of June, and Marfa, Texas was already in the full throes of summer. Right in the midst of this heat, besides the main group of actors, there were nearly 300 active stage personnel on hand to make movie magic happen. There were experts in lighting, makeup, and just about every other nuance of film imaginable at the beck and call of the director. There was even said to be a humongous wind generator used to simulate the turbulent dust storms of the West.

This cost millions of dollars, and with a price tag like that, the man in charge—director George Stevens—was determined not to fail. Stevens was in his early fifties at the time and had a long resume of experience at his disposal. He was also very thorough. He employed a system in which he would have multiple cameras capture footage of each scene from several angles so that when production made it to the final editing phase, he could choose the absolute best perspective of each shot.

Some greatly admired Stevens approach, but others detested it. Dean was in the latter camp. To him, Stevens often seemed like an overbearing taskmaster more than anything else. For Dean, Stevens was trying to organize everything into a neat little box, and his free-spirited approach was not something that could be easily cataloged and choreographed. Dean bitterly complained at the time, "When an actor plays a scene exactly the way a director orders, it isn't acting. It's following instructions."

For Dean, if there was not any adlibbed free exchange from the actors, it came off as stale and boring. Free-range acting was the formula that Dean had developed for success, and this freedom of thought was what had garnered him so much acclaim for *Rebel Without a Cause*. But Stevens was a detail-oriented controller when it came to his productions, and he wasn't about to hand over his hard-earned reins to James Dean and let him run the show.

This stance took a toll on Stevens' relationship with Dean, and the actor, who was already well known for his wild mood swings, was cold if not outright hostile to Stevens during the rest of the production. Rather than seeking direction from the director of the film, Dean was more likely to consult dialogue coach and former rodeo cowboy Bob Hinkle. Dean and Hinkle developed a deep friendship, and Hinkle taught Dean everything he knew about the rodeo—a valuable asset since he was playing a ranch hand—and soon Dean could ride and rope like an expert.

And even though Dean was not able to make any major alterations of the script, he still managed to get some nuanced flair into the dialogue by utilizing his newfound talent. He demonstrated this during a scene with Rock Hudson that would have been nothing but dry dialogue had Dean not spontaneously grabbed a rope and effortlessly went through a complex rope trick while they spoke. It was a minor gesture in the scheme of things, but it made Dean feel like he had at least a small amount of control over how the character was presented.

The cast of the *Giant* wrapped up filming in Marfa on July 8 and then departed for a studio in Burbank, California to lay down the final scenes of the movie there. At this stage of the production, Dean was working 12-hour shifts, arriving at the studio as early as 6:30 in the morning to begin work. But even though he was showing up early, he didn't always get screen time. Instead, he observed his co-stars Elizabeth Taylor and Rock Hudson getting to finish their takes, while he was being sidelined.

Growing incredibly impatient with the pace of things, Dean decided to boycott the film completely, refusing to show up until more of an effort was made to get him onboard. Realizing that one of their main stars was missing from the production, a panicked call was made to Dean's residence, and he was finally convinced to come back. And by late September, James Dean finished his contributions to the film. With his theatrical duties taken care of, Dean turned his attention once again to racing.

He booked himself for a spot in a major race being held in Salinas, California, scheduled for September 30,

1955. When the day finally arrived, Dean hopped into his Porsche along a mechanic named Rolf Wutherich. His friend, Bill Hickman, and Sanford Roth, a publicity photographer, followed in a separate vehicle, all heading to the race track. Dean hadn't driven the car much since he began filming for the *Giant* and was determined to break it in.

He barreled down the road at high speed during their trip, catching the attention of police on a couple of occasions, resulting in a fine and a stern warning to take caution. It was shortly after this warning that another motorist pulled out in front of Dean and his entourage. Dean hit the brakes but was going too fast to prevent a collision, and his car slammed head on into the other vehicle, launching the Porsche into the air where it flipped, rolled, and ultimately crashed into a telephone pole.

Dean's passenger, the mechanic Wutherich, was ejected from the vehicle and left with a broken jaw and hip upon slamming back down into the ground. Dean, on the other hand, was trapped, twisted, and mangled within the crumpled wreckage of the car. With his chest flattened, his neck snapped, and limbs contorted like a rag doll's, Dean was barely recognizable. Other motorists had witnessed the horrific accident and attempted to render aid, but it was clear to all who saw James Dean that this was a scrape from which he would not recover.

Dean then participated in one final high-speed race, this time inside an ambulance speeding off to the hospital, but as everyone already imagined, it was too late. And

James Dean, the eternal rebel and the king of cool, was pronounced dead soon thereafter.

The final respects and funeral service for James Dean were held on October 8, 1955, in his hometown of Fairmount, Indiana. It was an incredible scene with thousands of people converging on the steps of Friends Church, the same house of worship that Dean had attended as a young child.

Conclusion

There is an oft-repeated phrase in the world of celebrity: "art imitating life." But in the case of James Dean, you could easily argue that his was an instance of life imitating art. He became famous for playing the quintessential rebel in *Rebel Without a Cause*, but in truth, James Dean was a rebel from the very day that he was born. He never put much stock in the stringent rules of society and always sought to live life on his own terms.

He couldn't be pegged down into one category or classification. James Dean was a law unto himself. It was this headstrong vitality that was captured so perfectly on the big screen. To this very day, those in the throes of their youthful angst, and even some a little bit older, can identify with Dean's freewheeling and freethinking outlook on life. The electric charm of James Dean can still galvanize audiences all over the world. And as it turns out, this rebel has a cause after all.

Made in the USA
Las Vegas, NV
21 May 2023

72350272R00026